Introduction—Naeem's Story
A Dream Come True

Insomnia isn't usually a problem for me, but I tossed and turned throughout the night, too excited to slow my racing mind. Tomorrow I would be resigning from my job as a principal engineer at Honeywell Research Center—the firm at which, fresh from Brown University with a degree in electrical engineering, I had worked for five years. My career so far had been an exciting and fast-paced ride; I had received five promotions and taken on more responsibility each year. I had made a great start in my professional life, but the idea of starting my own company was just too compelling. I wanted to create something new; besides, I had always coveted the title "Vice President of Engineering" and was desperate to see it on my business card. Now, at the ripe old age of 27, I was about to fulfill my ambition.

Five of us, all engineers at Honeywell and Sperry Univac, had been working together for six months. The frozen tundra that is Minneapolis in midwinter offered the perfect environment in which to hole up inside as we worked on our brainchild during the nights and weekends from January through April. As engineers, the idea of developing customized computers that could streamline our jobs designing complex electronic circuits was exciting. Electronic design automation was a new industry—so new that it didn't even have a name yet. Such programs were simply called computer aided design (CAD) tools.

The big day eventually arrived. On May 15, 1985 I became Employee Number One and VP of Engineering at XCAT, our new company. Six months of nighttime and weekend product development had led us to believe that we had a fairly good idea of what we wanted to do and how the business would run. We even managed to attract an angel investor, who agreed to fund us for ten months by providing $50,000 each month in return for a small equity stake. The investor also agreed to let us use his abandoned warehouse as the startup's headquarters.

Within one month of our official founding date, we had about ten people working in the warehouse. The pace was feverish! We worked seven days a week, and a 14-hour day was considered a short day. Colleagues looked at you strangely if you tried to leave by 10 p.m.

Our extended hours and tireless effort, however, paid off. Loud cheers greeted the machine as it computed the correct outputs on the screen for the first time. We could not have been more exhilarated. The date was July 17, 1985.

A Dream Shattered

Fast forward two years. Things were very different. By this time, there were 44 employees in all, and we had assembled en masse in the company's large conference room. The purpose of our meeting: to announce the layoff of all but six employees, the firing of most of the management team, and the installation by investors of a new CEO who knew nothing about the industry or the product on which we had worked so hard.

We were divided into two groups and placed in two separate rooms. After a few minutes, it was announced that everyone in Room One had been terminated. A very small team remained in Room Two; their sole job would be to sell the company's assets. I was a member of this team.

What had happened? How could a team of bright young entrepreneurs be shut down so unceremoniously? After all, we were aces in our field and had worked assiduously to create a product that attracted customers in a burgeoning industry. What had we done wrong?

Our Mistakes

In our excitement and enthusiasm—not to mention our naiveté—we made a few basic mistakes, the same mistakes that many startups make:

- We focused on a product that we wanted and knew about, rather than one that potential customers wanted.
- We neglected to speak to potential customers or users.
- We had no idea whether there was a market big enough to support our product.
- We had no grasp of marketing or sales, and our concerns about secrecy kept us from seeking expert advice.
- We did not validate any of our key assumptions in the market.

TWELVE REASONS WHY BUSINESSES FAIL

1. Solving a problem that most users are not willing to pay to solve your way.

2. Thinking that you can do it all by yourself (without a founding team).

3. Lacking trust among team members—and not addressing the issue.

4. Being overconfident or dogmatic and not questioning yourself.

5. Lacking a crisp, singular focus—trying to be everything to everyone.

6. Marketing myopia: not having the vision to anticipate changes in the marketplace.

7. Confusing a hobby with a business.

8. Pricing incorrectly and not knowing your real competition.

9. Failing to properly define your market and customers.

10. Not having enough cash or financial resources available.

11. Focusing on a market segment too small to sustain you and the others in it.

12. Starting a business for the wrong personal reasons.

Lessons Learned

This book will examine these questions and offer to you the wisdom distilled from the dozens of lessons I have learned in my years as an entrepreneur—lessons learned by working at another five startups after XCAT, advising countless other startups, helping to start over a dozen more companies, and mentoring hundreds of fellow entrepreneurs. The nuggets of wisdom I'll share will help you avoid the mistakes I made and set you on a path much more likely to result in success than the one I followed early in my career.

Just a few weeks of homework could have saved the XCAT team a lot of heartache, opening the door for us to become a successful company with long-term staying power. We were woefully uninformed; we had no idea how important it was to consult users and buyers, since we were users ourselves and thought we had an up-close-and-personal grasp of everything that the market wanted. We never sought the advice and guidance of mentors or experienced businesspeople. In short, we made nearly all of the business mistakes possible—and we paid dearly for them. That is why I have written this short book: to help others avoid these very costly errors. Along the way, I will address the many issues and questions that beleaguer entrepreneurs looking to start their own business.

The cost of failure for a startup business is high. You will invest both time and money into your business and, if your business fails, you will have wasted all of it—unless you learn from your mistakes and create a stronger business as a result.

 ## THE COST OF FAILURE

People often do not realize how expensive it is, in more ways than one, to start a business. Usually people commit anywhere from one to three years of their lives to starting a business. The cost of being underemployed during this period can total several hundred thousand dollars. The hard costs—the monies that you will spend on equipment, personnel, and fees—are significant, not to mention the "soft costs"—the toll that starting a business takes on your health and relationships. These costs must not be underestimated. For this reason, I believe that every entrepreneur should talk seriously with his or her loved ones and seek their support before diving into a new venture. The costs can be worth it, but it is vital that you do some computation before you start.

This ebook asks a few basic questions that will significantly increase your chances of success in business. These questions are what I call the *"7 Steps to a Succesful Startup."* If you spend time answering these questions over the next few weeks, you will jump to the front of the line of entrepreneurs striving to set up a successful business. The seven basic steps I outline in this book will prepare you for the realities of startup life before you quit your day job and jeopardize your family's income. Most entrepreneurs are so excited about their business idea that they skip this essential preparation and are devastated when their business fails. Don't be one of them! There will come a point when launching yourself headlong into your venture and leaving behind your old income source will be inevitable. If you follow my seven-step method, you will be able and ready to identify that point precisely and seize your opportunity.

There are no two ways about it: starting a company is challenging. But the huge mortality rate of business startups is linked, more than anything else, to a lack of clarity, planning, and preparation. In launching a business, planning and preparation are vital: they separate potential success from potential failure. This book enables you to gain that clarity and plan for success.

It's Not All Doom and Gloom

The failure statistics are frightening, and may well put you off the idea of being an entrepreneur and setting up your own business. Indeed, starting a business is scary and stressful! But the entrepreneurial life offers huge benefits. You make your own rules. You own your own company. You develop your own strategies and see them through. Most gratifying of all, you pursue the things you desire at your own speed. It is incredibly satisfying to create something from scratch and watch it transform from a startup to a successful business with hundreds of employees. True entrepreneurs have a passion for making things happen. Let's get to it!

1

Portrait of an Entrepreneur—
Are You One?

Most people think of an entrepreneur as a risk taker—someone who is reckless and impulsive, perhaps even a gambler. Having been around thousands of entrepreneurs, and being one myself, I have never considered entrepreneurs to be reckless risk takers—just the opposite, in fact. A true entrepreneur works constantly and always does due diligence to maximize the odds of success. Entrepreneurship is a state of mind. It involves the ability to see around corners, to imagine and predict what is possible, and to organize these thoughts into an execution plan. A true entrepreneur will then act upon this plan to make things happen. Most people are able to perform the first two steps, but the majority fall short when it comes to the third step, the execution phase.

> 46% of workers at large companies agreed that their job interferes with personal and family needs; only 31% of small-business employees said the same.
>
> *Harris Interactive, September 2006*

The Characteristics of an Entrepreneur

Having met many successful entrepreneurs, and having worked with or mentored many of them, I have noticed that they all share the following characteristics:

1) **They are comfortable "living in fog."** Many people simply cannot live or make decisions without the clarity offered by empirical data. It is just too hard for them to make decisions based only on a little data and a gut feeling. But this is often exactly the type of move demanded of an entrepreneur. I call this approach "living in a 40-70 zone"—making decisions with at least 40% but usually no more than 70% of the data normally required for action. In a large corporation, it would be considered reckless to make decisions with so little information. Large companies are, as a result, often slow to act, since they must collect a great deal of information before making them and then create consensus around the decision.

> 62% of entrepreneurs in the U.S. claim "innate drive" as the number one motivator in starting their business.
>
> *Northeastern University's School of Technological Entrepreneurship, October 2006*

2) **They are able to assemble a team of people to follow them.** Very rarely does a solo founder create something of value. Almost without exception, more than one person is behind a great company. If an entrepreneur's vision cannot convince at least one other person to join him or her, then perhaps the vision is not so fantastic.

3) **They show persistence and determination.** It takes persistence—a key quality in an entrepreneur—to make any idea stick. Persistence should not, however, be confused with stubbornness.Stubbornness is a failing. It can make you dig in your heels and cling to an idea that's better released. Entrepreneurs are always listening for and using the data they receive to tweak their ideas until an idea morphs into something fundable, something that gains traction.

All ideas must be chiseled away at in order to make them viable.

4) **They have conviction.** True entrepreneurs are good at paying attention to trends and adjusting their thought processes accordingly. Such flexibility is always balanced with a healthy dose of conviction; nothing is gained by bending your ideas to every conversation you have. That would be exhausting!

5) **They have passion.** Entrepreneurs have a passion for an idea and are not put off by the prospect of hard work. Without true passion, an entrepreneur would give up at the first obstacle. Passion motivates the entrepreneur.

Entrepreneurs are a bit like a sculptor at work; they start with a slab of marble which, over time, with skill, passion and hard work, is shaped into a beautiful thing.

A true entrepreneur works constantly on ideas, chiseling away at them until they are working and fundable. I have never seen an idea go to market as originally conceived; an entrepreneur's ideas evolve, and he or she often shapes them while speaking with customers, users, buyers, and influencers. These in-process innovations may relate to the market, to technology, or to the chosen business model. Successfully refining an idea requires that the entrepreneur remain open-minded, willing to amend ideas based on conversations with real-life potential users. We will talk more about how to collect this data later.

> **Successful entrepreneurs are very stubborn about their vision, but extremely flexible about their vision's execution.**

2

Essential Preparation Steps for Every Entrepreneur

If you want to succeed, a certain amount of preparation must take place before starting a new venture. Smart entrepreneurs make these preparations before quitting their day job because doing so reduces the risk inherent to the endeavors they are about to undertake.

 More than 70% of early-stage entrepreneurs are already employed workers.

GEM, January 2006

Your investors and employees will expect you to have completed this phase of planning and preparation, and *you*, more than anyone, must find the answers to certain questions before taking the plunge and chasing your dream.

I will walk you through these steps to your success—the planning that will clarify your thinking before you dive headfirst into a new idea. In my experience, less than 10 percent of the people who come to me proceed with their original idea after completing these steps.

I suggest that you start this seven-step preparation program while you are still employed, in school, or doing whatever else you usually do. You will only be ready to launch into the business properly after you have completed these essential steps, which can take anywhere from three to six months. They can be completed more quickly, but I have never seen them require less than two months—and it can take much longer than that. Don't rush and do a sloppy job; each step is vital. Isn't the future success of your business worth spending some time to plan properly now? This period of preparation is, in my opinion, the most important part of any project you will undertake as an entrepreneur.

 TAKE NOTE:

After completing these steps, you will be in a position to write a business plan. You won't, however, be ready to launch your business yet. Usually another phase, one to six months long, commences after the initial preparations are complete. During this phase, you will write a business plan and raise money, and only then launch the business.

3

The 7 Steps to a Successful New Venture

My 7-Step program consists of seven basic questions that you must able to answer before creating your business. I will walk you through each question, showing you how to get the answers you need to move on to the next one.

Let's look at these seven basic questions that every would-be entrepreneur should ask. I have intentionally numbered the first question Step Zero, since it is unique among the questions and is so fundamental to your success.

0) Why do I want to do this?
1) What is the unmet need?
2) How big is this opportunity?
3) Who else is trying to meet this need? What about our approach is different and unique?
4) How will I make money (who will pay me)?
5) Why us?
6) Why now?

Some of you may find these seven questions very pedestrian. You may wonder how they Jibe with the business books you have read. Translating these seven essential questions into MBA jargon might make them more meaningful to some of you:

0) Am I clear about my personal and professional motivations?
1) What market shall we target?
2) What is the market size?
3) What is the competitive landscape and what is our differentiated market positioning?
4) Do we have a scalable business model?
5) Do we have a team with the right experience, vision, and commitment?
6) What about market dynamics makes NOW a good time to act?

At the end of the day, in whatever form you phrase these questions, they must be clearly fixed in your mind. Answering these questions will require significant preparation, including:

- Research
- Soul searching
- Conversations with real potential customers and users (these groups may not be the same!)
- Conversations and discussions with partners and your team

Addressing each of these six topics (not including Step Zero, about which I will speak in the next chapter) requires conversations with real people, not just Internet research. That is why this process takes weeks to complete. You will find, however, that it is worth every minute.

4

Step Zero

There is a preamble to this preparation. I call it *"Step Zero,"* and it is a vital step if you really want to be an entrepreneur. Entrepreneurship is not for everyone; you may find out during Step Zero that such a life is not really what you want. But it is better to find out now, before you lose money, time, and sleep over your business.

In Chapter One, *"Portrait of an Entrepreneur,"* we discussed some of the attributes of an entrepreneur. Do you have these attributes? Think carefully. Being an entrepreneur is incredibly satisfying, not just financially (and not always financially!), but also at a deep personal level. It is a lifestyle and a mind set.

Go back to Chapter One and read it again. Look deeply into yourself. Are you a true entrepreneur? Think, too, about your family. Will your wife/husband/partner be happy about this dramatic life change?

Don't move on to Step 1 unless you are sure that being an entrepreneur is for you. Are you really ready for this journey?

I strongly advise people who come to me to get away for a weekend so that they can think through this question without being interrupted by people or the noise of TV, iPods, and mobile phones. Take a hike in the forest and think through the above issues one by one. If you come back still committed to the idea and the journey, then get ready to start on the remaining six steps.

5

Step 1—
What is the Unmet Need?

Every business venture should seek to satisfy an unmet need, a "pain point" for customers. In other words, every business should offer something that prompts people to part with their hard-earned money, either to solve a problem or to fulfill a desire.

Sometimes the need is not obvious; some entrepreneurs, like Steve Jobs of Apple, are able to see "around the corners" to fill a need people never knew they had. At other times, the need is staring everyone in the face, but no one has been able to fulfill it in a way that adequately meets the customer's needs, that solves the problem well enough. The completeness of your solution is important to the viability of your idea. Innovation can occur in other aspects of a product than its technology: it can take place in a business model or purchasing method. Case in point: software-as-a-service (SaaS), in which customers can use software by logging onto the Web rather than storing all of a program's data on their own computers or servers. Customers pay as they use these services, significantly reducing the cost of installing and maintaining expensive software.

The most successful startup businesses identify a need and then provide a solution, rather than coming up with an idea and then trying to find a market for it. A good example of a business idea that satisfies a preexisting need is one of the big search engines, such as Yahoo!, Alta Vista, or Google. When the Internet first came into being, it seemed miraculous: there were tremendous amounts of information on it, and the world was quite literally at the user's fingertips. The problem was that it was hard to find the right information. Search engines offered a solution to this pain and frustration, making it easy to find the right information. They met a need with a solution. Furthermore, they created a compelling and effective model for advertising to users, as they knew precisely what these users were searching for.

 Don't make assumptions. Always validate your beliefs.

Entrepreneurs can usually identify this unmet need through research. Observe people's behavior; think about and identify what can be done to make their lives easier, simpler, more efficient, or more productive. The best ideas usually come from deep domain knowledge— expertise in a certain field. Many entrepreneurs, however, make the key mistake of not talking to enough people to validate what they believe. *Don't make assumptions. Always validate your beliefs*. Validation is an essential part of identifying this unmet need. Here are several techniques you can employ to this end:

1) **Talk to people**—Talk to several people (ideally several dozen people) and describe the area in which you seek feedback. Follow the method below to gather and document what you hear. You need to be sure that you really are homing in on an unmet need, so talk to enough people to satisfy yourself of this fact.

2) **Perform a simple survey on the Internet**—All it takes is a short survey of less than 10 questions. Several companies, inclu-ding **www.surveymonkey. com** or **www.zoomerang.com**, offer a free account for two to four weeks. Take advantage of it!

Don't confuse users with customers. They are often the same people, but sometimes they are not. In healthcare, for example, the users of a product may be doctors or nurses, but the customer (the one who decides to purchase) is usually a CIO (Chief Information Officer) or a CTO (Chief Technology Officer) or another administrator. You must talk to both users and customers and ensure that the solution you plan to offer meets their unmet need or simplifies their life in some significant way.

3) **Employ some students or freelancers** to talk to users or customers on your behalf, once you have done a few interviews and figured out a set of questions that will clarify the picture for you. Do not delegate the first few interviews to others, however; do these yourself, because you need to get a personal feel for the market.

When you talk to people, don't start by telling them what you are thinking about. Instead, ask how they are living without your invention.

What data are you seeking?

When you talk to people, don't start by telling them what you are thinking about. Instead, ask how they are living without your invention. Ask them what alternatives they have considered and why they have not used one of these alternatives. Listen to their answers and ask probing questions in response. This second and third layer of clarifying questions—I call it "peeling the onion"—will help you to understand their thought processes. It is essential that you dig deeply, burrowing beneath the rudimentary answers people usually give.

 Remember, your aim is to understand their need, NOT to tell them about your idea.

Write down what you hear and systematically record your observations. Remember, your aim is to understand their need, NOT to tell them about your idea. You can also ask some questions to learn about price points. Another clarification worth obtaining is how the solution would be purchased. In other words, if you were offering the ideal solution to a particular problem:

- Who would buy it?
- What is their company title?
- How much can the purchaser spend without approval from a department head or boss?

All of this data will be essential for you as you perform market research and formulate your product. Later, it will inform your pricing and launch strategy.

Every once in a while, I hear entrepreneurs saying, *"What if my idea is so unique and revolutionary that no one can give me any meaningful feedback on it?"* I usually find, after I have helped the entrepreneur think through this question carefully, that almost all ideas fill some need that is just waiting to be found. A little digging will reveal almost any need, whether previously recognized or not. If you are having trouble with this question, think harder—or send me an email at naeem@startup-advisor.com. I will be sure to include any exceptions to this claim in this book's next edition.

I once did this type of "onion peeling" homework and discovered that the electronic switch we were designing would be purchased by an IT manager in Japan—not by a CTO (Chief Technical Officer) or a VP (Vice President) of Engineering, and certainly not by an engineer. We also discovered that this IT manager could usually spend up to $5,000 without having to obtain departmental approvals. Guess where we priced our product once it was launch-ready, and guess toward whom we targeted our marketing messages? You guessed correctly: we marketed to the IT manager, and sold the switch at a price point of $4,800.

6

Step 2— How Big is This Market?

Why should you chase big markets? How big is big enough? How do you even calculate the size of a market, especially when it may not yet exist? The entrepreneurs that I advise often ask these questions, which I will address in this section.

Market size is the sum of all of the revenues of all of the companies serving your target market segment ("target market segment" simply means the portion of the market at which you are aiming your product or service). You must define your market segment correctly in order to size it correctly.

 MARKET SIZE

Market size is simply how much people spend (or are likely to spend) every year to buy the kind of product you are creating to solve their problem. Research the prior growth rate in your chosen market to predict its future growth rate, unless you can better identify or justify what your growth rate will be based on new trends or demographics, new buying habits, or other changes. Always look for "proxies"—examples of how other companies in your target market succeeded—so that you can justify your assessments.

Market Size Examples

Let's suppose that you have an idea for developing an innovative supply chain management company that delivers medications more efficiently to long-term care facilities. What is the size of your target market? Well, the overall healthcare market in the U.S.A. is in the trillions of dollars, and the medications market alone is almost $300 billion, but the long-term care segment in the medications market was about $14 billion in 2006 and is growing steadily. If you dive further into this market segment, you may find out that the medications being supplied by pharmacies to long-term care facilities still constitute a $7 billion-plus market (the rest may be supplied by mail-order companies or by clinics and hospitals). So the correct answer for your target market is $7 billion, growing at a rate of 15 percent due to the growth in the elderly population and the continuously increasing amount of medication being consumed.

ANALYZING YOUR MARKET

A bottom-up analysis starts with the product and then takes into account the number of users and how often they buy. A top-down analysis looks at the total market first and then works down to look at your market segment. I encourage you to start with a bottom-up analysis and only use top-down numbers for a sanity check. If your bottom-up numbers tell you that you can sell to 1.4 million users within four years and then you find out that only 2 million users exist, you will know that you are unlikely to gain a (1.4/2x100 =) 70% market share of anything in four years. These numbers should send you back to the table to evaluate your assumptions about the bottom-up analysis.

Let's look at another example. What if you make software that helps truckers and logistics companies improve fleet management? Well, the trucking industry overall is worth well over $400 billion in annual sales, but your segment is much narrower than that. The sum of all software revenue to these companies may only be $2 billion. It is important to identify what market you plan to target; it needs to be defined as specifically as possible. Now, you may plan initially to make just one type of software, but you also plan to add additional modules and optimize the software for efficient fleet management and back-haul optimization. You will need to estimate how much of this $2 billion is being spent on the types of problems you intend to address within two to four years. *That* will provide your target market size.

What if you are making instruments for left-handed dentists? Well, your total market size will be based on how many such dentists exist and, given your price point, how often they replace these instruments. Knowing these answers will help you to gauge an annual market size.

You should always do a "bottom-up analysis" to compute market size. Later, you can do a "top-down analysis" to make sure that your initial computation is reasonable. For example, if your bottom-up analysis on the market for your dental instrument yielded a number of $300 million per year, and you later discover that the total market for these instruments for all dentists in the USA is $500 million, then you know something is wrong with your calculation and analysis. Left-handed dentists are unlikely to make up 60% of all dentists in the U.S.!

Plenty of opportunity exists to start companies that target smaller markets, but you either have to be very accurate in your marketing or such a specialist in that market that others are put off from entering it and competing with you. Typically, a billion dollars or more is a good-sized market that will enable you to attract a significant number of investors. This doesn't mean you shouldn't aim at $200-million or $300-million markets; it just means that it may be harder for you to find investors in those markets. Naturally, different rules and numbers will apply if you are starting a small business and you intend to serve the local market or a highly specialized niche market. Just know your target market and sizes, and be aware of your maximum revenue potential given the market size.

MARKET SIZE MATTERS!

Hitting your target market is just like hitting a dart board positioned across the room—you will have to be very precise (or very, very lucky) to hit it. But if someone asked you to hit any part of that wall from across the room, you'd be able to do it with your eyes closed. Market size is just the same. If you target a small market, you will have to be correct and precise in almost all of your decisions in order to hit that market. If you target a large and growing market, you can be wrong a number of times and still capture a piece of that market.

Venture capitalists (VCs) like to invest in companies targeting a market approaching $1 billion or larger, or a fast-growing market that will achieve that size within three to five years. The reason for this is simple: a VC wants to reduce his or her risk by investing in a company with a greater likelihood of making money!

7

Step 3—Can We Create Differentiated Market Positioning?

or Who Else is Trying to Meet This Need, and What About Our Approach is Different and Unique?

Step 3 is all about understanding your differentiated market positioning—in other words, what makes you or your product or service different from other companies offering similar products or services within your target market.

 If your only differentiation is price, then you should be very worried.

To understand the dynamics of your market, you must do thorough research. You must consider who is serving your chosen need already, today, and how you plan to meet and serve this need differently. Research the current market, making note of your competitors, their products, and the like. To succeed, you must be different in some way, offering one or moreof the following:

- Better quality
- A cheaper price
- Easier to use
- New capabilities
- A new way of buying

Something must differentiate you from other companies and provide a reason for people to buy from you. Buyers and consumers need to be able to put you in a different compartment from other providers of a similar solution to their unmet need. My least favorite attribute in the above list is price. If your only differentiation is price, then you should be very worried. It is quite easy for a competitor to lower their price in order to put you out of business, and then raise their price again once you are out of the picture. You'd be better served think of other, more compelling differentiators.

This step is also a good time to find out whether potential buyers even value your differentiation. If your differentiator is that you offer a product in multiple colors, you will be in trouble if your target market doesn't care about color choice!

When asked, *"At what age do you think it would be too late to start your own business?"* 60% responded, *"Never too old."*

Yahoo! Small Business/Harris Interactive, April 2006

True, sometimes a product is so innovative and new that users cannot imagine it and so cannot provide any useful feedback. This does happen, but far less often than people think. When this happens, you must do something to ignite your user's imagination so that you can gain some type of feedback. Why not write a press release or a product brochure so that you can show it to potential customers? You could even make a prototype, conduct a demonstration, or commission an artist's rendition so that you can elicit a reaction from potential buyers and users—anything to obtain feedback. Making a prototype or having a brochure printed will be far cheaper than developing the product and launching it with the idea of surprising your market!

When seeking feedback from customers, don't just listen to their words; watch their body language and observe their reactions. Figure out what they really mean by their answers, and use probing questions to find out more.

> Making a prototype or having a brochure printed will be far cheaper than developing the product and launching it with the idea of surprising your market!

No Competition

I always greet the claim *"But we have no competition"* with suspicion. Usually there is some type of competition. Put yourself in your customer's shoes and think about where they would presently go to have their need met. There is always an alternative to your product or service. And don't forget: not buying and doing nothing are both viable—and common—alternatives for your customers!

You should also take into account the fact that existing companies are always redeveloping products and creating new ones, so be aware that your competition may at this moment be working on a product that will compete with yours.

THE ART OF POSITIONING

Positioning is the real estate you would like to occupy in your customer's mind. How will they think of you? Positioning must be precise and narrow, a reality that makes many entrepreneurs very uncomfortable. They hate being confined in a small niche, since they are convinced that they can be so much more to so many more people. This type of thinking is a dangerous trap! If users and customers cannot put you into a tidy compartment in their brain, they are unlikely to remember you at all. Be precise. *"We make pediatric surgical instruments for left-handed dentists"* is a precise positioning statement. *"We do IT services,"* is a horrible positioning statement, as thousands of companies can claim the same thing. *"We set up secure online stores for small booksellers"* is a much better positioning statement.

8

Step 4—How Will I Make Money and Who Will Pay Me?

This step of preparation deals with understanding your business model. You need to think about and clarify the following:

- Who is the customer?
- Out of whose pocket is the money coming out of?
- How does the money get from them to me?

These questions are fundamental, but they may not be simple to answer. I have come across many entrepreneurs who could not. But you most certainly need to know these answers before you start.

You must question, research, and understand how people buy in your chosen industry. Consider the following:

- How will I reach those customers?
- What is the cost of acquiring and serving each customer?
- What will be the cost of training?
- What is the cost of servicing each customer?

The answers to these questions should factor into your decisions and determine whether your chosen service or product is a good business for you. If it takes professional service to serve each customer, your ability to scale rapidly will be greatly limited. For example, suppose that you were going to sell a device that required installation and training for each customer. How many people would you, as a small startup business, be able to train and support in a month? Wouldn't that limit your ability to scale? What if you used a channel partner trained by you, and they then supplied and trained the final customer? Would that change your ability to scale? Yes, but consider what portion of your sales price the channel partner would command.

How do I know whether my business is scalable? you may ask. A business is scalable if the cost of serving the next ten customers is dramatically less than serving the first ten customers.

All of the above are the types of questions that must be researched before you start. A few phone calls and discussions with channel partners, as well as other companies who use such channels, will answer many of these questions for you.

Each market has established methods for how people buy the product, and trying to change user behavior is not as easy as you may think. It is possible, but will require significant resources—more resources than you may have. An example is Apple's iTunes, which changed the business model for how music is purchased. Buying one new song at a time via one's computer was a revolutionary concept—one that took hundreds of millions of dollars and the full marketing muscle of Apple to convince people to adopt. Can you afford the time and money to convince people of such a groundbreaking business model?

 USERS MAY NOT BE CUSTOMERS:

You also must remember that the end user of your product is not always the customer. For example, perhaps you are selling hands-free, voice-activated communications devices so that nurses and doctors can call or page each other without having to use their hands. The users will be nurses and doctors, but the actual buyers are usually the IT department or the CIO of the hospital. You will have to think about how to get both of these groups on board with your idea. Not having this clarity can cost you significant time and business.

Understanding Channels:

How the product travels from you to the end user is important to understand. You have three main choices:

a) **Direct Sales:** Selling directly means hiring sales people and directly approaching customers to make sales. This approach is typically used for complex products where customer intimacy is required. It is an expensive way to start selling.

b) **Indirect Sales or Distribution:** This approach involves training distributors and/or resellers who then interface directly with customers. There can be several layers involved in this approach, and each industry is different.

c) **Web-Direct Sales:** The Internet opens up the possibility of a global marketplace, and selling goods and services directly to consumers through the internet has lowered the cost of selling dramatically. You still have customer acquisition costs and marketing costs, but the internet does offer a compelling way to sell to your customers.

A bigger issue is whether your business model is scalable. Why should you care about scalability? Because it will directly impact your ability to create a large and profitable company. For a law firm, the cost of serving each customer requires additional bodies that limit scalability. However, for YouTube, the cost of serving the next video poster is infinitesimally small when compared to the cost of serving the very first video. Once the servers and infrastructure were in place, YouTube could easily serve more and more customers without incurring a proportional amount of additional cost, making their business model potentially very scalable and profitable. The same applies to other Internet companies such as eBay. On the other hand, a restaurant business or a barber shop is not so easy to scale: in the restaurant business, food must be bought and cooked for each new customer, while a barber must spend the same amount of time cutting the hair of each new customer. Franchising can give the owners of such businesses the opportunity to scale, but these businesses are in general less easily scalable than internet-based businesses.

Scalability = Higher profitability

High Profitability =

Less Work, More Money

A COSTLY MISTAKE—
NOT UNDERSTANDING
THE BUSINESS MODEL

In one of my startups, we invented the world's first silicon fingerprint sensor chip. This tiny device can now be seen on many laptops; users touch it (or swipe their finger across it) to log in to their machines. We found out the hard way that a complex supply chain was involved in buying this product and incorporating it into a laptop. It was not at all clear to whom we should sell this device. We were approaching banks and online retailers and offering them a secure way to transact business online, all to no avail. We did not realize that these companies do not buy fingerprint sensors from startups—they buy secure transaction solution from a company like IBM or EDS, who then buys authentication solutions from a security solutions provider, who in turn buys from a biometrics authentication company. We needed to be selling to such a biometrics solution provider.

9

Step 5—
Why Us?

This question will be on any venture capitalist or investor's mind. It should also be on yours. Ask yourself, *"What is it about us as a team that will allow us to succeed in this venture?"* This question is a very serious one, and you must be able to answer it properly. **Possible answers can include:**

- We have been working in this field for seven years, so we really know where the treasure is buried and what customers want. We use competitors' products every day, and we know what to do better.

This is not a bad answer. Domain knowledge (knowledge of your field) is always very valuable. I often see somebody who is not from a particular field come up with bright ideas about how to improve a product; the problem is that the person lacks domain knowledge. I am all for "outside-the-box" thinking, and sometimes you do see things in a new light when unburdened by insider knowledge. In general, however, it is always smart to respect somebody's domain knowledge—so if you are not a domain expert, at least surround yourself with people who have spent a fair amount of time in your target product domain.

Another answer may be:

- We have agreed to work with the professor who invented this technology and wants us to commercialize it.

  or

- We recruited two advisors with deep domain knowledge who will advise us. We also have youthful energy and are completely committed to seeing this idea through; as well, we have already invested over three months in researching it.

These are all possible good answers. How good they are will depend on the particular situation, but you must be able to tell investors why your team is uniquely qualified to pursue your chosen idea.

The Importance of Teams

Have you noticed that I have been using the term "team" and not "founder" or "entrepreneur"? The reason for this is simple: few, if any, examples exist of a single person starting a successful venture and scaling it. Such a task is just too big for one person to be able to do well. Also, if you cannot convince at least one other person (preferably two) of your vision, then perhaps you don't have such a compelling vision—in other words, a vision that will successfully attract investors and customers. Naturally, if you are starting a small business rather than a scalable venture, it is possible to do it alone with a single founder (businesses such as a shop, a cleaning service, or some import or export businesses). I am focusing my comments, however, on ventures intended to scale to millions in revenues within five years, ventures intended to provide significant returns to their investors.

You may think that Microsoft and Apple were started by solo entrepreneurs, but that's not true. Microsoft was started by Bill Gates AND Paul Allen, and Apple was started by Steve Jobs AND Steve Wozniak. You need someone, preferably more than one person, to share the load, to support you and work with you on this immense task.

Always start your business by recruiting a team. The joy of startups is in creating a functional team composed of members who have diverse strengths and skills and unique experiences to draw from. At least one member of the team should have deep domain knowledge (knowledge of the target market and its dynamics).

The old adage *"two heads are better than one"* is worth remembering. A team can bounce ideas off of and support one another. Fresh eyes looking at a problem or obstacle can often provide a solution that no one else had thought of.

Your team should include:

- You
- Other like-minded entrepreneurs who are also passionate about the product or service and join you as co-founders
- A board of advisors

A team does need a leader. This leader may or may not be you. The leadership may shift over time, or you may bring on another manager (or a CEO) if the company gets to such a stage.

If you don't have a team, don't start the business. You need to have two or three cofounders before you can get the show on the road. Working with like-minded people will be a satisfying experience, make the work easier, and prime you to attract investors.

**FOUR GOALIES
DO NOT MAKE A TEAM**

A team, by definition, must contain people with different skills who bring different point of views to the table. I have observed that the best teams are those in which team members have a deep respect for each other's core competencies—a respect that usually comes from having worked together before.

Making a Founding Team

What makes a good team? People who like each other, people who have been friends for years, people who have worked together in the past? No single definition definition applies to every case, but I have observed that the best teams are those in which team members have a deep respect for each other's core competencies—a respect that usually comes from having worked together before.

At times there will be strong disagreements, and working in a team is not always easy, but deep respect for each other's capabilities usually overcomes these types of issues. Complementary skills are essential to forming a good team; ideally, your team should contain people with expertise in selling, technology, finance and marketing, and business development. Not all team members have to be on board at the same time; they can be brought on over time when needed. And remember: the cofounder title is an honorary one. Early employees are not necessarily automatic co-founders.

10

Step 6—
Why Now?

SOLUTIONS

Correct timing is key. *"Why now?"* is a question that you must be able to answer. Perhaps a regulatory change has made your product or service idea plausible now, or perhaps the price of a component or product has fallen, enabling you to reach a new audience. Perhaps a new standard has been announced or agreed upon that makes the timing right. You may not have a clear answer, but you should strive for as much clarity as possible about why this idea makes sense at this moment and why somebody did not think of it two years ago. You may discover some new and revealing facts.

If people have tried to create a business with your product or service in the past, what made them fail? Research this question, so that you can be sure either that 1) your idea is different, or 2) something about the market makes "now" the right time.

A couple of examples of changes that can make "now" a good time for certain types of businesses are: the new WiMax deployment in certain countries, which has brought the cost of broadband access to under $10 a month; and the formation of a new Homeland Security department, which allows security-related technologies access to funds.

Unless you consider the question *"Why now?"* you are likely to repeat mistakes that have already been made. Maybe there are serious technological, logistical, political, or regulatory hurdles that will make it hard for anyone to succeed, never mind a small startup company. That does not mean that you should not try, but you do need to prepare yourself for challenges by asking this question and finding a satisfactory answer to it.

 WHY TIMING MATTERS

Your potential investors will have this question on their mind, so you must satisfy both yourself and them with an answer. Why is NOW a good time to do this? What changed? The answer could be technology evolution, macro trends, consumer sentiment, or some breakthrough. But whatever it is, you must think about it and be prepared to speak to it with data.

11

The End—
Or Is It the Beginning?

We've reached the end of the seven steps of preparation that will give you and your startup a greater chance of success. Try to work five to fifteen hours a week on this preparation while you are still employed at your day job. This planning and preparation phase will take a few weeks to complete (I have seen this process take anywhere from one to six months), although it can be done more quickly if you work on it full-time.

The output, your planning, may consist of a single page for each of these seven questions, or it may run several pages for each. Length doesn't matter, as long as you have satisfied yourself and your team with your answers to the questions. This work forms the start of your business plan, which is the next step in your journey.

WHEN TO FORM A
LEGAL ENTITY

I am often asked this question. Most people start by forming a legal entity of some kind, a step that I feel is often premature. You need such a formal structure only once you are ready to accept investors' money or are about to start selling something. I suggest that you save your money until then and use signed paperwork and personal memoranda to document agreements. All of these can be formalized once you are ready to incorporate; then you can identify the type of legal entity that is best for your business. Read websites from your area's Secretary of State and Small Business Administration Bureau for further clarification on these topics.

12

How Will I Know
When I Am Ready?

You will be able to tell when you are ready to dive in and start the business once you have satisfactory answers to the basic questions I have talked about in this book.

Think about the following:

- Do I have a burning passion?
- Am I knowledgeable about my idea?
- Do I know why I want to do this?
- Is my idea unique and different?
- Is there a market for my idea? Are people spending money to solve or address the pain/ need that I intend to address?
- Is the market big enough?
- Do I have validation for my idea? Have I talked to enough people?
- Do I have a team assembled?

The above questions work like a filter, enabling you to analyze your ideas and identify the good ones. Excellent ideas will pass through all of the filters, while bad or mediocre ideas will get stuck somewhere along the way and have to be thrown out. These filtering questions will save you precious time and resources.

From past experience with many startups, I can guarantee that following these steps will make you far more prepared to start your new ventures. Your planning and preparation will shine through in your dealings with potential customers and investors, and your work will pay off. You will have differentiated yourself from the majority of startups, and the odds of success will be dramatically shifted in your favor.

> Starting a company or your own business is a very satisfying experience. It is so much more than just making money or pursuing a career; it is a journey of self-discovery. Bon voyage!

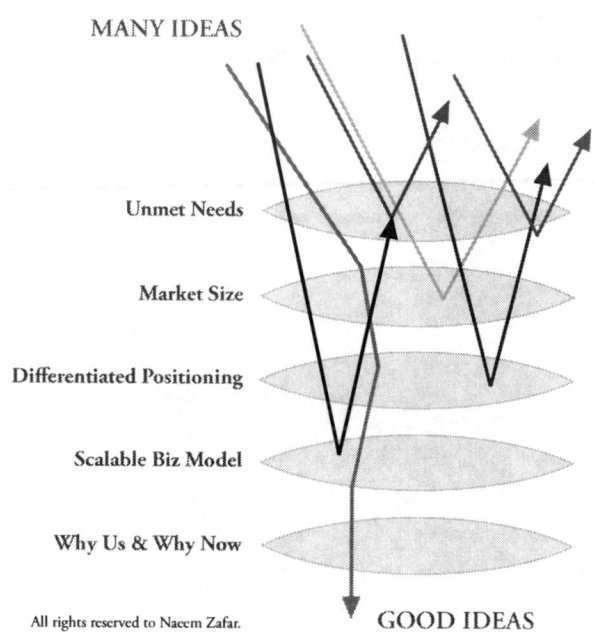

MANY IDEAS

Unmet Needs

Market Size

Differentiated Positioning

Scalable Biz Model

Why Us & Why Now

GOOD IDEAS

13

Epilogue

I hope that this book serves as a useful checklist for you as you venture into starting a company or joining a startup. Starting your own business is an exciting, enriching process: you will learn much about yourself and it will be a very rewarding journey, whatever the end result.

I plan to write several additional e-books to help you with other questions that will arise— questions about raising money, hiring and recruiting talent, go-to-market strategies, and managing your board and investors. This learning works best when it is shared, so I invite you to write to me and share your stories, advice, and ideas. In this way, others may benefit from your insight and experiences.

Please write to me at **naeem@startup-advisor.com**. I look forward to meeting you at one of my seminars or clinics very soon.

NAEEM ZAFAR

About the Author

NAEEM ZAFAR is a member of the faculty of Haas Business School at the University of California, Berkeley, where he teaches Entrepreneurship and Innovation as part of the MBA program. He has also lectured on business, innovation, and entrepreneurship at UCLA, Brown University, Dalian Technical University in China, and Lahore University of Management Sciences (LUMS) in Pakistan.

Naeem is a serial entrepreneur, having started his own business at the age of 26 and gone on to start or work at six other startups. He has extensive experience as a mentor and coach to entrepreneurs and CEOs, and is the founder of Concordia Ventures, a company that educates and advises entrepreneurs and startups on all aspects of starting and running a business.

Naeem most recently served as president and CEO of Pyxis Technology Inc., a company specializing in advanced chip design software for nanometer technology. He has also been president and CEO of two other technology startups, Silicon Design Systems and Veridicom (a Bell Labs spinoff that invented the silicon fingerprint sensors today found on most laptops). Naeem has held senior marketing and engineering positions at several companies, including Quickturn Design Systems, which had an IPO in 1993 and grew to $125M in revenues.

Naeem obtained a Bachelor of Science degree (*magna cum laude*) in electrical engineering from Brown University in Rhode Island, and he also has a master's degree in electrical engineering from the University of Minnesota. Naeem is a charter member of TiE (The Indus Entrepreneurs, **www.TiE.org**) and a charter member of OPEN (**www.OPENSiliconValley.org**), where he serves as a member of the executive committee. Naeem also holds several other board positions, including Numetrics Ltd., Brainstorm Pvt. Ltd., and Aanukaa Inc., and enjoys serving on the advisory boards of five other companies. As a part of his global entrepreneurial practice, Naeem is involved with microfinance ventures and social entrepreneurship in Pakistan (Rural Asia) and Mexico (CREA).

Naeem's experience in starting his own businesses, as well as advising hundreds of entrepreneurs and dozens of startups, puts him in a unique position to help others succeed.

To contact Naeem about sharing your own experiences, or to give feedback about this book please email him at naeem@startup-advisor.com.

Naeem has written several other books that will be helpful for anyone starting a business or wanting to scale it. For more information on these books please visit www.Startup-Advisor.com.

CPSIA information can be obtained
at www.ICGtesting.com
Printed in the USA
FSOW01n0307090417
32861FS

9 780983 314905